50 Little Paper-Pieced Blocks

Full-Size Patterns to Mix & Match

Carol Doak

Text copyright © 2011 by Carol Doak

Photography and Artwork copyright © 2011 by C&T Publishing, Inc.

Publisher: Amy Marson

Creative Director: Gailen Runge

Acquisitions Editor: Susanne Woods

Editor: Liz Aneloski

Technical Editors: Carolyn Aune and Gailen Runge

Cover/Book Designer: April Mostek

Production Coordinator: Jenny Leicester

Production Editors: Alice Mace Nakanishi and S. Michele Fry

Illustrator: Kirstie Pettersen

Photography by Christina Carty-Francis and Diane Pedersen of C&T Publishing, Inc., unless otherwise noted

Published by C&T Publishing, Inc., P.O. Box 1456, Lafayette, CA 94549

Acknowledgments

Many thanks are extended to my husband for his support throughout my quilting years and to the staff at C&T Publishing for their support, encouragement, and friendship.

Dedication

This book is dedicated to all those quilters who share love and friendship through quilting.

Contents

Gallery of Blocks

Fan (page 14)

Tree (page 14)

Star 1 (page 15)

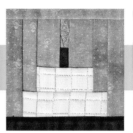

Birthday Cake (page 15)

Heart 1 (page 16)

Heart 2 (page 16)

Shamrock (page 17)

Feature Square (page 17)

Birdhouse (page 18)

Crocus (page 18)

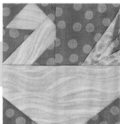

Duck (page 19)

Crazy-Patch Easter Egg (page 19)

Cross (page 20)

Umbrella (page 20)

Sailboat (page 21)

Bluebird (page 21)

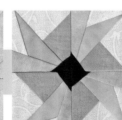

Pinwheel (page 22)

Twin Flowers (page 22)

Sunrise (page 23)

Radiant Star (page 23)

Starburst (page 24)

Lily (page 24)

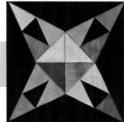

Star 2 (page 25)

Hot Air Balloon (page 25)

Airplane (page 26)

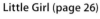
Little Girl (page 26)

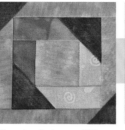

Rosebuds (page 27)

Mailbox (page 27)

Funky Tree (page 28)

Star 3 (page 28)

Love (page 29)

Basket 1 (page 29)

Star 4 (page 30)

Flowerpot (page 30)

Flower Trellis (page 31)

House (page 31)

Crayons (page 32)

Framed Tree (page 32)

Maple Leaf (page 33)

Flag/Heart (page 33)

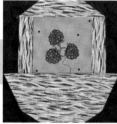
Basket 2 (page 34)

Christmas Flower (page 34)

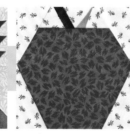
Apple (page 35)

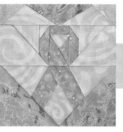
Heart/Ribbon (page 35)

Star 5 (page 36)

Dreidel (page 36)

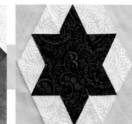
Six-Pointed Star (page 37)

Candle (page 37)

Tree Ornament (page 38)

Gift (page 38)

Introduction

I come from a family in which the creative arts are enjoyed, appreciated, and passed down through the generations. Therefore, it was an easy transition to incorporate my paper-pieced block designs into cards for family and friends.

I first began making cards for my mother for Christmas. Then I began making them at other times of the year. Mom always called right away to let me know the card had arrived and how special it made her feel to receive something made with such care.

When someone receives a card you have made, that person not only enjoys the sentiment that comes with the card, but also appreciates that you have taken such care to make a card especially for him or her. I enjoy making the cards because I know they will be received as something very special. I hope you too enjoy the process of making cards for family and friends and sharing something special with them.

Using the Blocks for Keepsake Frame Cards

Carol Doak's Keepsake Frame Cards are designed to hold a 3″ paper-pieced block design in a debossed cutout frame. The block design used can be specific to a season or holiday, such as the Tree Ornament or the Crazy-Patch Easter Egg, or it can be generic, such as a star. The tri-fold card is easy to use and can be oriented either vertically or horizontally. The block is centered in the cutout, the covering of the double-stick tape is removed, and the left side of the card is folded over the center. The quality of the paper used for the card and envelope is like that of handmade paper.

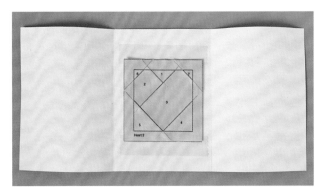

Center block in cutout area, remove tape covering, and fold left side of card over block.

You can stencil, stamp, and write messages to decorate the card. The Rubber Stamp Tapestry company (see Resources, page 39) offers a variety of stamps with words as well as alphabet and border stamps.

Another way to decorate a card is to stitch a decorative stitch on it. Use a heavy needle (90/14) and Size 40 thread, so the thread will not break while stitching. Do a stitch test on paper of a comparable weight before stitching on the card.

Using the Blocks for Fabric Projects

These wonderful little blocks also can be assembled to make coasters, table runners, small wallhanging quilts, pillows, tote bags, and embellished garments, to name just a few options—the possibilities are endless.

Introduction to Paper Piecing

Supplies

- Small stick-on notes to label fabric pieces
- Postcards or small pieces of card stock
- Carol Doak's Foundation Paper (by C&T Publishing)
- 6″ Add-A-Quarter and 6″ Add-An-Eighth rulers (by CM Designs)
- Flat-headed pins
- Neutral-colored sewing thread
- Rotary cutter and small mat
- Sewing machine, 90/14 needle, and open-toe presser foot

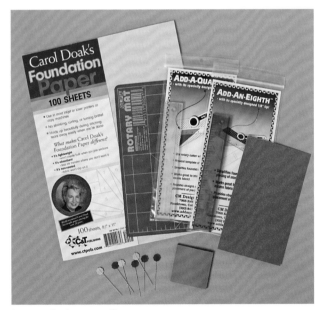

Paper-piecing supplies

Preparing to Paper Piece

1. Make 1 copy of the block foundation for the chosen block using an accurate copy machine and **Carol Doak's Foundation Paper**, or by tracing the pattern onto the paper using a pencil, ruler, and light source. Trim the foundation on the dashed line.

2. For each block, cut the fabric pieces listed in the cutting list and label each piece with its location number.

> **Notes**
>
> - Because there are many tiny pieces in these blocks, I oversized the cut sizes in some cases to make them easier to handle.
> - When you see ⧄ in the cutting list, that is the indication to cut a square and then cut it in half diagonally to make two half-square triangles. When you see ⊠ in the cutting list, that is the indication to cut a square and then cut it twice diagonally to make quarter-square triangles. Sometimes you will not use all the triangles that you cut.

3. Set up your sewing machine with neutral-colored thread, a 90/14 needle, and an open-toe presser foot (so you can see the needle as you sew on the line). Set the stitch length to 18–20 stitches to the inch, or 1.5 on a sewing machine that has a range of 0–5.

Step-by-Step Paper Piecing

1. Select the #1 fabric piece. Looking through the *blank side* of the foundation, place the fabric right side up over the #1 area. Turn the foundation over and confirm that the fabric extends at least ¼″ beyond the #1 area. Pin in place using a flat-headed pin placed parallel to and away from the #1/#2 seamline. Placing the pin this way will prevent you from accidentally sewing into a pin.

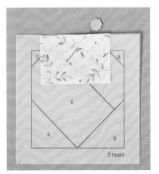

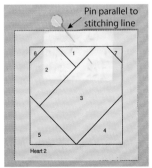

Place #1 fabric and pin.

2. With the lined side of the foundation facing up on the cutting mat, place a postcard on the line between pieces #1 and #2. (Plain card stock is used in the following photos so as not to be distracting.) Fold the paper over the edge of the card, exposing the excess fabric.

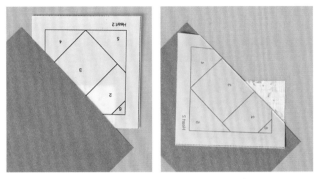

Place postcard on line and fold paper over card.

3. Place the Add-A-Quarter Ruler on the fold and trim the exposed fabric ¼" from the fold using the rotary cutter.

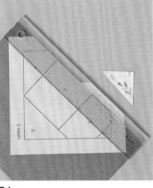

Trim.

> ### Note
>
> I use both the Add-A-Quarter and Add-An-Eighth rulers (by CM Designs) when paper piecing these blocks. When the fabric pieces are larger, use the Add-A-Quarter Ruler. When they are smaller or there are several seams merging to one area, use the Add-An-Eighth Ruler. For the example shown here, I used the Add-A-Quarter Ruler.

4. Place the #2 fabric right side up on the blank side of the paper over the #2 area, approximating the position for piece #2. Flip the #2 fabric over and place it right sides together with the edge of the #1 piece just trimmed. Adjust the placement along this line so it will cover the #2 area when it is sewn and pressed open. Pin in place.

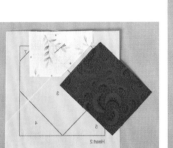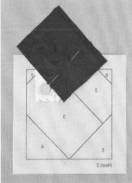

Place #2 fabric and pin.

5. Sew on the line between #1 and #2, extending the stitching about ½" at both ends.

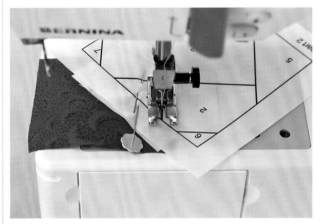

Sew.

6. Clip the threads and remove the pins. Press the #2 piece open with an iron on a cotton setting with no steam.

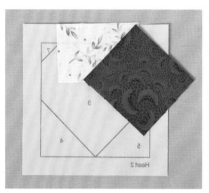

Clip threads, remove pins, and press.

7. Place the postcard on the next line you will sew. In this example, it is the seamline between #1/#2 and #3. Fold the paper back on the edge of the card. Because the previous stitching extends at the end where #3 meets, you will tear it away from the foundation, and that is okay. Place the Add-A-Quarter Ruler on the fold and trim the fabric from the seamline.

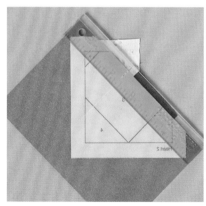

Place postcard, fold paper, and trim.

8. Position the #3 fabric in the same manner as you positioned the #2 fabric piece and sew on the line between #1/#2 and #3. Clip the threads and press open.

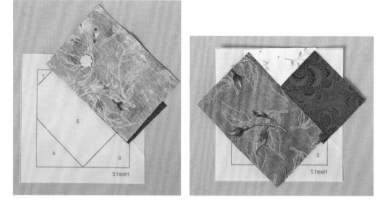

Position #3 fabric, sew, clip threads, and press.

9. The #4, #5, #6, and #7 pieces are half-square triangles. To position the triangle for #4, trim the #4 seamline ¼˝ from the fold as before. Place the #4 triangle right side up on the blank side to approximate placement. Flip it over and place it right sides together with the just-trimmed seam, aligning the corner of the triangle with the triangle printed on the paper. Sew on the line, clip the threads, and press open.

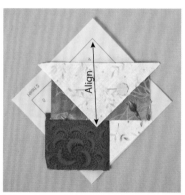

Trim #4 seamline, align #4 triangle, sew, clip threads, and press open.

10. Complete the block by adding the last 3 pieces.

11. To trim the block, place the ½˝ line on the rotary ruler on 2 adjoining sides of the square. Trim on the dashed trimming line of the foundation. The fabric will extend ½˝ outside the solid sewing line. Turn the block and trim the remaining 2 sides in the same way.

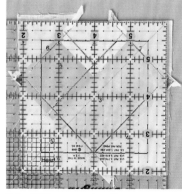

Trim ½˝ from sewing line.

Paper-Piecing Tips

Pieced Units

A few of the blocks contain pieced units. When you see a **//** across a seamline, such as the #8 piece in the Flag/Heart block, that is the indication that the pieces of fabric will be sewn together along that seamline off the foundation prior to joining the #8 pieced unit as a single piece to the foundation. In the photo, the pieced unit for #8 is pinned in place, with the

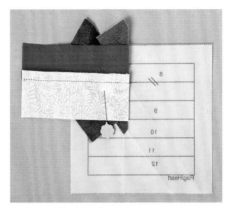

Position #8 pieced unit.

sewn seam positioned on the foundation seam. Then, it will be machine basted just across the seamline to check for placement prior to stitching the #8 piece in place.

Stitch, press open, align the seam on the line on the paper, and machine baste the opposite end of the pieced unit to the foundation, so it will not move.

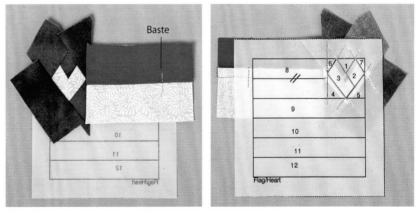

Machine baste opposite end.

When a **//** is placed across 2 seamlines, the 3 pieces are stitched together prior to adding the pieced unit to the foundation. This is the case for the Cross, Umbrella, and Tree Ornament blocks.

Blocks Made of Sections

Some of the block designs are made of 2 or more sections. The dashed lines along the joining seamlines are ¼˝ from the sewing line, rather than the ½˝ used on the outside of the block. Trim the blocks on the dashed lines. Pin the sections together at the ends and at any matching points. Set your sewing machine to a basting stitch and machine baste at the beginning, end, and any matching points. Open the seam to check for a good match. If the sections are not perfectly aligned, remove the basting stitches, readjust the sections, and rebaste. When you are happy with the match, sew the entire seam, using 18–20 stitches to the inch.

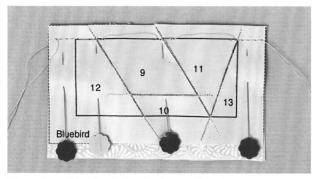

Pin and machine baste beginning, end, and matching points along seamline.

When joining a block with one or more seams that do not intersect, press the seams open from the fabric side to reduce bulk.

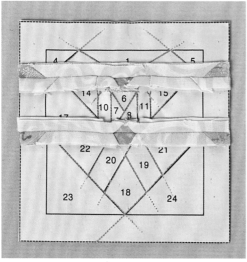

Press seam open to reduce bulk.

When joining blocks made from seamed units that intersect, such as 4-block rotations (see Pinwheel, page 22), press the seam allowances from the fabric side in opposing directions, so they will lock in place when you join the halves. After the blocks are joined, split the middle horizontal seam in the opposite direction. To split the seam, clip just a couple of stitches in the seam allowance and tear the foundation's seam allowance to open the seam up in the center.

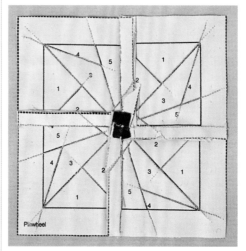

Press intersecting seams in opposing directions.

Center Fabric Elements

Blocks such as Feature Square (page 17) and Basket 1 (page 29) offer the opportunity to feature a fabric element in the #1 position to provide extra detail to the block. If you are sending a card for a very specific occasion, you are likely to find a printed fabric for that purpose that can be featured in the center square. Measure the area to audition fabric options. Cut the oversize #1 piece and position it in between the lines and paper piece.

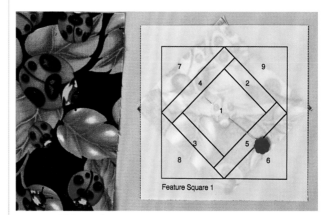

Featured fabric element in #1 position

3″ Block Designs

The following 3″ finished block designs are placed in the order they might be used throughout the year. Remember that the Gift block (page 38) could be made in baby colors for a baby gift and Basket 1 (page 29) or Basket 2 (page 34) could be worked in spring colors for an Easter basket. The Featured Square block can feature just about any design for any time of year or any occasion. Many of the designs will have generic applications.

The cutting lists provided for the blocks are created on the premise that you will be making one block at a time, so the oversized fabric pieces can accommodate several locations in the block. The ◹ symbol indicates to cut a square and then cut it *once* diagonally to make half-square triangles. The ⊠ symbol indicates to cut a square and then cut it *twice* diagonally to make quarter-square triangles. There are times when you will have a triangle left over, so don't be concerned if that happens.

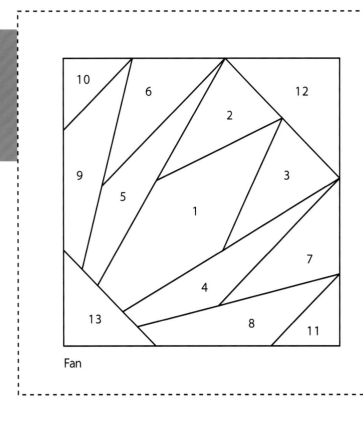

Fan

Fabric	Number to cut	Size to cut	Location
Black	1	2¾″ × 2¾″ ◩	12
	1	2¼″ × 2¼″ ◩	10, 11
	4	1½″ × 3″	2, 3, 6, 7
Medium red	2	1¼″ × 3½″	4, 5
Dark red	1	2½″ × 2½″ ◩	13
Dark teal	1	1¾″ × 3½″	1
Light teal	2	1¼″ × 3½″	8, 9

◩ Cut squares; then cut them in half diagonally.

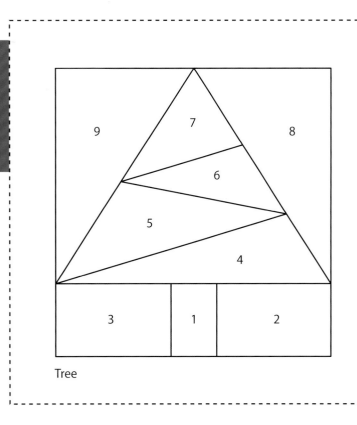

Tree

Tree

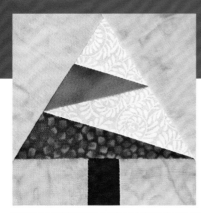

Fabric	Number to cut	Size to cut	Location
Blue	2	2¼″ × 4½″	8, 9
	2	1½″ × 2″	2, 3
Brown	1	1¼″ × 1½″	1
White	2	1½″ × 3½″	5, 7
Green 1	1	1½″ × 4″	4
Green 2	1	1¼″ × 2¾″	6

Star 1

Fabric	Number to cut	Size to cut	Location
Navy	8	1¾″ × 2½″	1, 4
Purple	4	1½″ × 2½″	5
Gold	4	1¼″ × 2¼″	3
Light blue	4	1″ × 2″	2

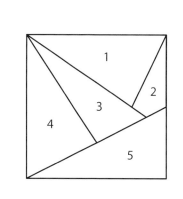

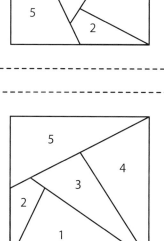

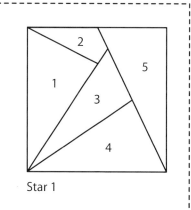

Star 1

Birthday Cake

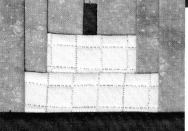

Fabric	Number to cut	Size to cut	Location
Yellow	1	1″ × 1½″	1
Light blue	2	1¼″ × 2″	7, 8
	5	1¼″ × 3¾″	10, 11, 13, 14, 15
	4	1″ × 1½″	2, 3, 4, 5
White	2	1¼″ × 3″	9, 12
Dark blue	1	1″ × 3¾″	16
	1	1″ × 1″	6

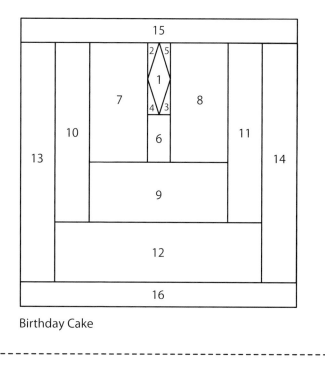

Birthday Cake

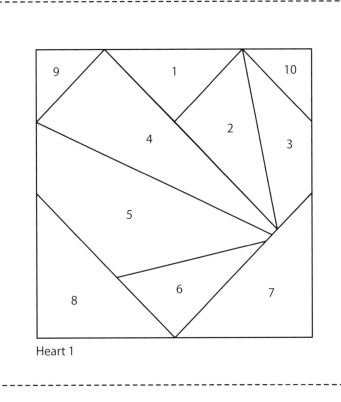

Heart 1

Heart 1

Fabric	Number to cut	Size to cut	Location
White	1	3″ × 3″ ◹	7, 8
	1	2¼″ × 2¼″ ◹	9, 10
	1	1½″ × 2½″	1
Assorted pinks	1	2″ × 2¼″	2
	2	1¾″ × 4″	4, 5
	2	1½″ × 3″	3, 6

◹ Cut squares; then cut them in half diagonally.

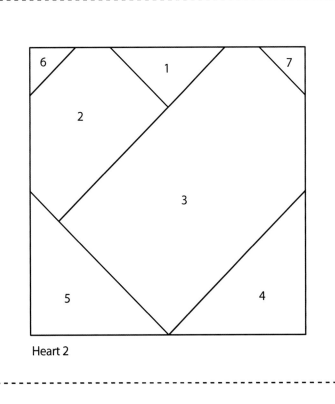

Heart 2

Heart 2

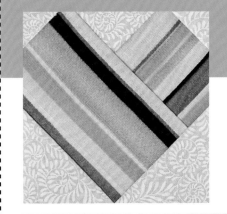

Fabric	Number to cut	Size to cut	Location
White	1	3″ × 3″ ◹	4, 5
	1	2″ × 2″ ◹	6, 7
	1	1½″ × 2″	1
Stripe	1	2½″ × 3½″	3
	1	2″ × 2½″	2

◹ Cut squares; then cut them in half diagonally.

Shamrock

Shamrock - A

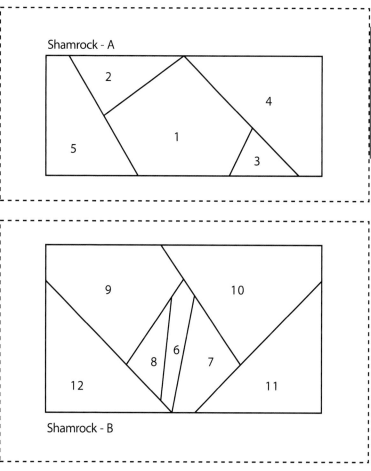

Shamrock - B

Fabric	Number to cut	Size to cut	Location
Light green	1	3″ × 3″ ◩	11, 12
	2	2″ × 3½″	4, 5
	4	1½″ × 2″	2, 3, 7, 8
Assorted medium greens	3	2½″ × 2½″	1, 9, 10
	1	1″ × 2″	6

◩ Cut square; then cut it in half diagonally.

Feature Square

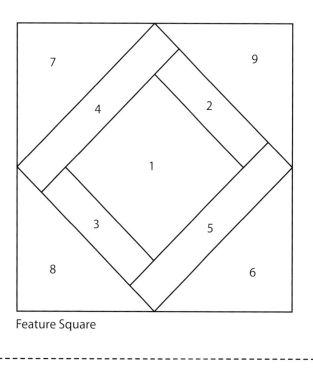

Feature Square

Fabric	Number to cut	Size to cut	Location
Floral	1	2¼″ × 2¼″	1
Green	4	1″ × 3″	2, 3, 4, 5
Yellow	2	3″ × 3″ ◩	6, 7, 8, 9

◩ Cut squares; then cut them in half diagonally.

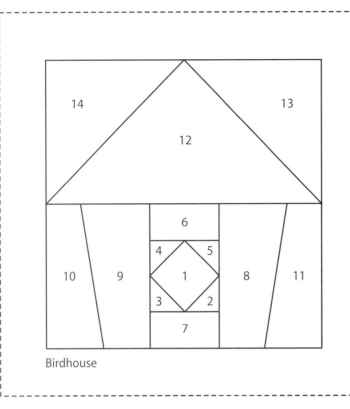

Birdhouse

Birdhouse

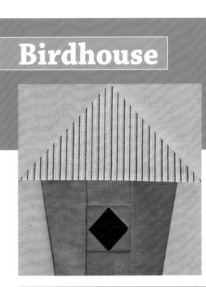

Fabric	Number to cut	Size to cut	Location
Yellow	1	3″ × 3″ ◳	13, 14
	2	1½″ × 2½″	10, 11
Green	1	2¼″ × 3¾″	12
Teal	2	2″ × 2″ ◳	2, 3, 4, 5
	2	1½″ × 2¼″	8, 9
	2	1″ × 1½″	6, 7
Black	1	1¼″ × 1¼″	1

◳ Cut square; then cut in half diagonally.

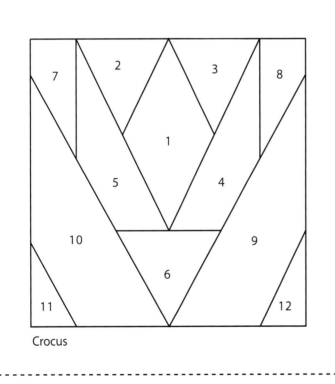

Crocus

Crocus

Fabric	Number to cut	Size to cut	Location
Floral	6	1½″ × 2½″	2, 3, 7, 8, 11, 12
Yellow	1	1¾″ × 3″	1
Light purple	2	1¼″ × 3″	4, 5
Medium purple	1	2″ × 2″	6
Green	2	1½″ × 4¾″	9, 10

Duck

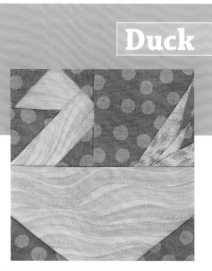

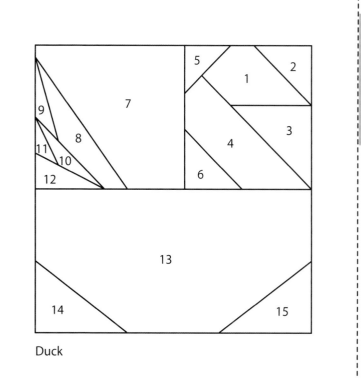

Duck

Fabric	Number to cut	Size to cut	Location
Blue	2	2½″ × 2½″ ◺	2, 3, 5, 6
	1	2½″ × 2½″	7
	2	1¾″ × 3″	14, 15
	2	1″ × 2″	9, 11
Yellow	1	2½″ × 4″	13
	2	1½″ × 2½″	1, 4
Gold	3	1″ × 2¾″	8, 10, 12

◺ Cut squares; then cut them in half diagonally.

Crazy-Patch Easter Egg

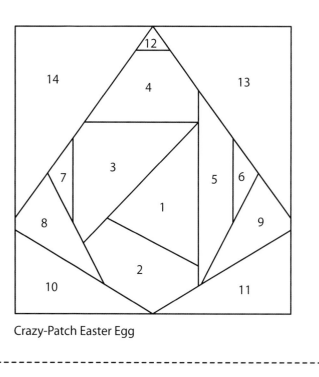

Crazy-Patch Easter Egg

Fabric	Number to cut	Size to cut	Location
Floral	2	2¼″ × 4½″	13, 14
	5	1½″ × 2¼″	6, 7, 8, 9, 12
	2	1¾″ × 3″	10, 11
Assorted solids	5	1¾″ × 3″	1, 2, 3, 4, 5

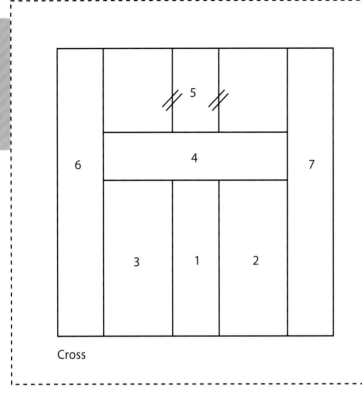

Cross

Cross

Fabric	Number to cut	Size to cut	Location
Gold	2	1¼″ × 2¾″	1, 4
	1	1″ × 1¾″	5
Medium blue	2	1½″ × 2½″	2, 3
	2	1½″ × 1¾″	5
Light blue	2	1¼″ × 4″	6, 7

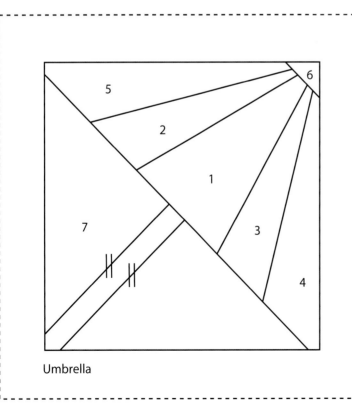

Umbrella

Umbrella

Fabric	Number to cut	Size to cut	Location
Assorted fabrics	5	2″ × 3½″	1, 2, 3, 4, 5
	1	2″ × 2″ ◩	6
Blue	1	3½″ × 3½″ ◩	7
Gold	1	¾″ × 3½″	7

◩ Cut squares; then cut them in half diagonally.

Sailboat

Fabric	Number to cut	Size to cut	Location
Sky	6	1¼″ × 2½″	2, 4, 7, 8, 10, 11
	2	1½″ × 3″	12, 13
Water	1	2½″ × 2½″ ◨	15, 16
Black	1	1″ × 3″	5
Assorted greens	2	1¼″ × 3″	6, 9
Red	1	2″ × 4″	14
Rose	2	1¼″ × 1¾″	1, 3

◨ Cut square; then cut it in half diagonally.

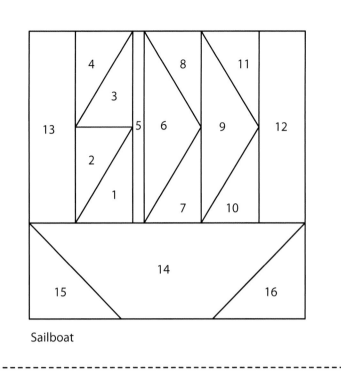

Sailboat

Bluebird

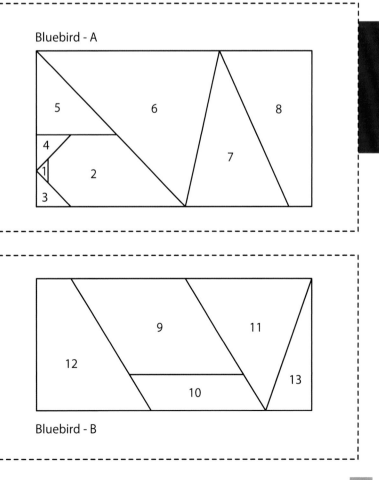

Bluebird - A

Bluebird - B

Fabric	Number to cut	Size to cut	Location
Yellow	1	1″ × 1″	1
Light blue	2	2½″ × 2½″ ◨	3, 4, 5
	5	2″ × 3½″	6, 8, 10, 12, 13
Medium blue	2	1¾″ × 2½″	2, 9
Medium-dark blue	1	2″ × 2½″	7
Dark blue	1	2″ × 2½″	11

◨ Cut squares; then cut them in half diagonally.

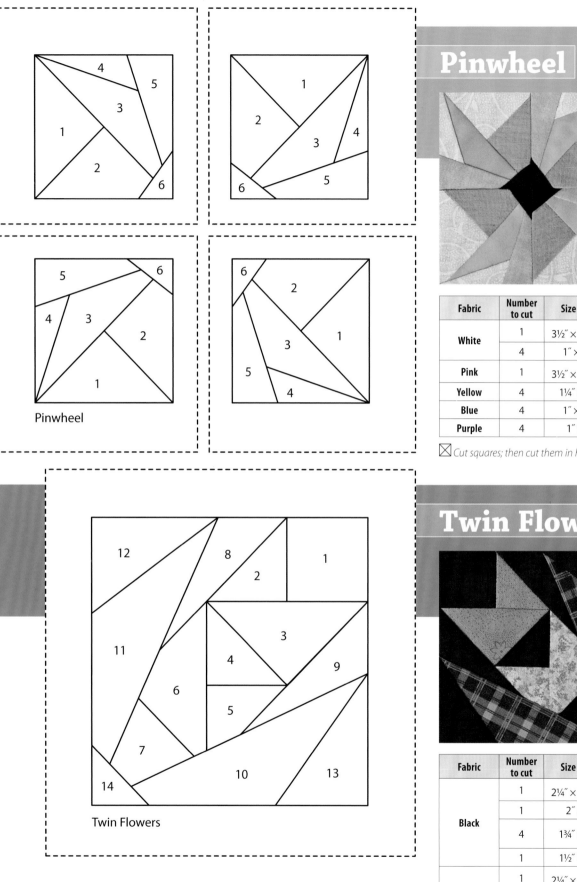

Pinwheel

Twin Flowers

Pinwheel

Fabric	Number to cut	Size to cut	Location
White	1	3½″ × 3½″ ⊠	1
	4	1″ × 2¼″	4
Pink	1	3½″ × 3½″ ⊠	2
Yellow	4	1¼″ × 2½″	3
Blue	4	1″ × 2¼″	5
Purple	4	1″ × 2″	6

⊠ Cut squares; then cut them in half diagonally twice.

Twin Flowers

Fabric	Number to cut	Size to cut	Location
Black	1	2¼″ × 2¼″ ◻	4
	1	2″ × 2″	1
	4	1¾″ × 3½″	8, 9, 12, 13
	1	1½″ × 1¾″	7
Green	1	2¼″ × 2¼″ ◻	14
	2	1½″ × 4″	10, 11
Blue	1	2½″ × 2½″ ◻	2, 3
Purple	1	2½″ × 2½″ ◻	5, 6

◻ Cut squares; then cut them in half diagonally.

Sunrise

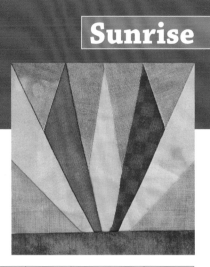

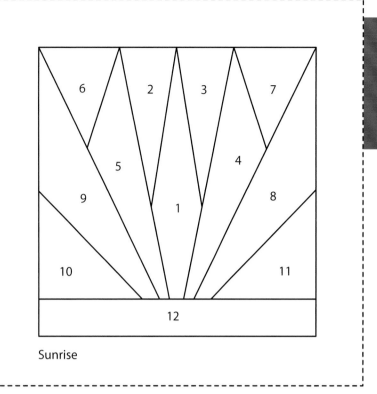

Sunrise

Fabric	Number to cut	Size to cut	Location
Light blue	1	2¾″ × 2¾″ ◩	10, 11
	2	1¾″ × 2½″	6, 7
	2	1¼″ × 2¾″	2, 3
Green	1	1¼″ × 4″	12
Assorted red, orange, yellow	5	1¼″ × 4″	1, 4, 5, 8, 9

◩ Cut square; then cut it in half diagonally.

Radiant Star

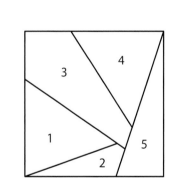

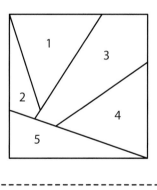

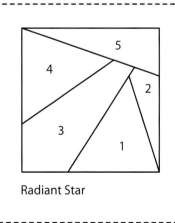

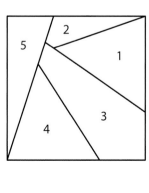

Radiant Star

Fabric	Number to cut	Size to cut	Location
Yellow	8	2¼″ × 2¼″	1, 4
White print	4	1¼″ × 3″	3
Blue print	4	1¼″ × 3″	5
Blue check	4	1″ × 2″	2

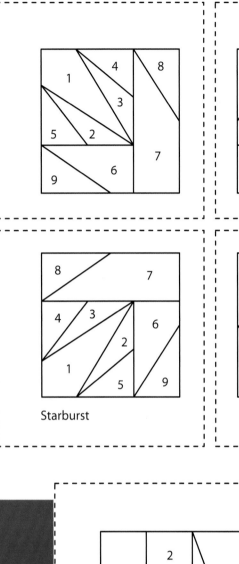

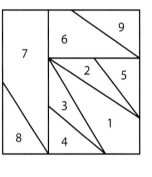

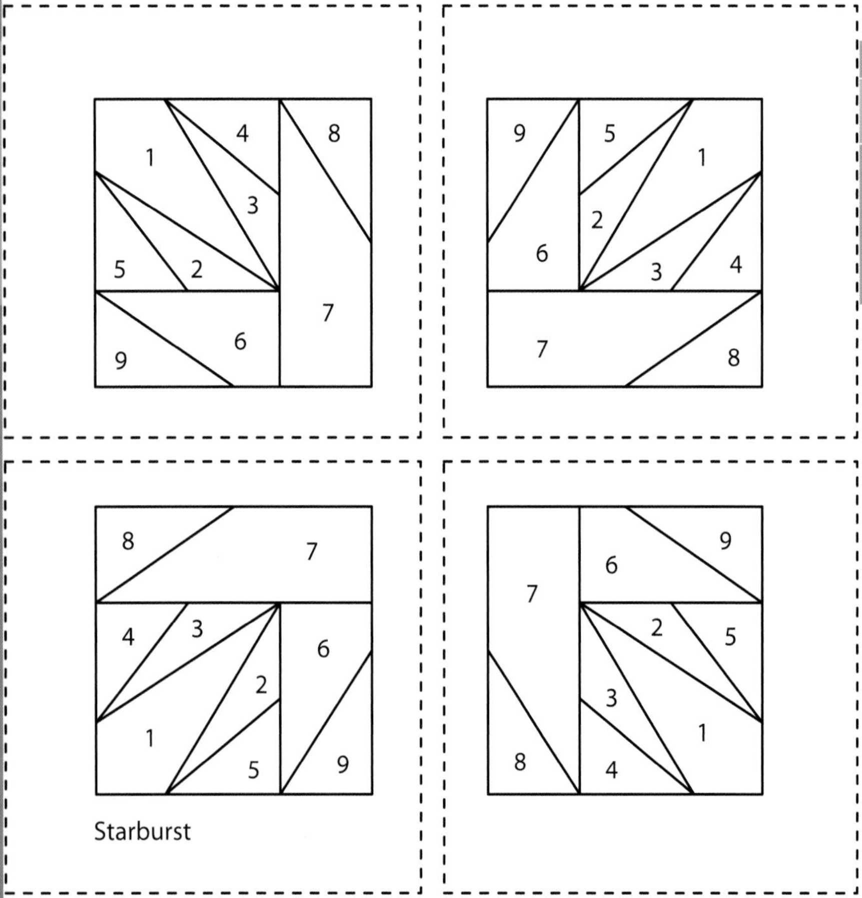

Starburst

Fabric	Number to cut	Size to cut	Location
White	4	1¼″ × 2½″	1
	16	1¼″ × 2″	4, 5, 8, 9
Medium green	4	1¼″ × 2½″	7
Light green	4	1¼″ × 2″	6
Assorted pastels	8	1″ × 2″	2, 3

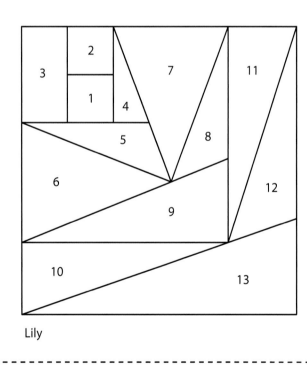

Lily

Lily

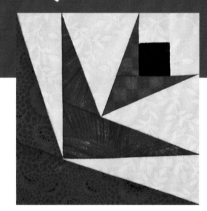

Fabric	Number to cut	Size to cut	Location
White	4	1¾″ × 3½″	6, 7, 10, 11
	2	1½″ × 2″	2, 3
Black	1	1¼″ × 1¼″	1
Red 1	2	1½″ × 2½″	4, 5
Red 2	2	1½″ × 3½″	8, 9
Red 3	2	2″ × 4¾″	12, 13

Star 2

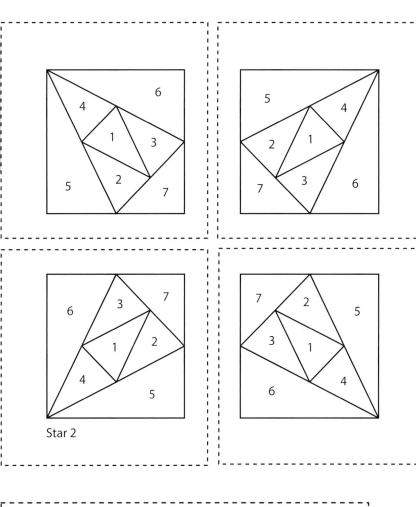

Star 2

Fabric	Number to cut	Size to cut	Location
Black	8	1½″ × 3″	5, 6
	4	1½″ × 1½″	1
Assorted solid colors	2*	2¼″ × 2¼″ ◹	7
	12	1¼″ × 2″	2, 3, 4

*Or use 4 different colors as pictured.

◹ Cut squares; then cut them in half diagonally.

Hot Air Balloon

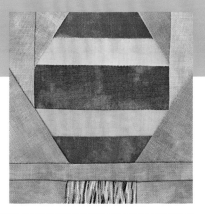

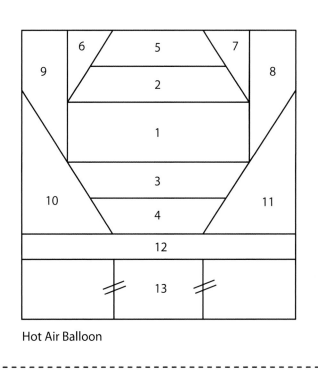

Hot Air Balloon

Fabric	Number to cut	Size to cut	Location
Blue	2	1½″ × 3″	10, 11
	4	1½″ × 2½″	6, 7, 8, 9
	2	1½″ × 2″	13
	1	1½″ × 4″	12
Beige	1	1½″ × 1½″	13
Green	1	1¼″ × 2¾″	1
Yellow	2	1″ × 2¾″	2, 3
Pink	2	1″ × 2¼″	4, 5

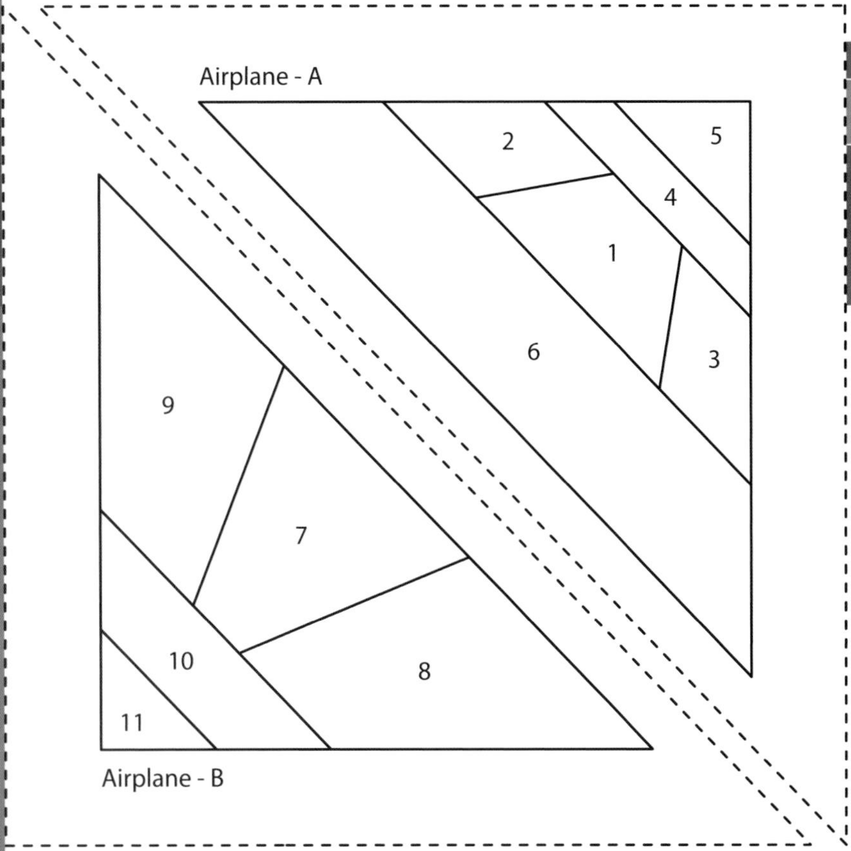

Airplane

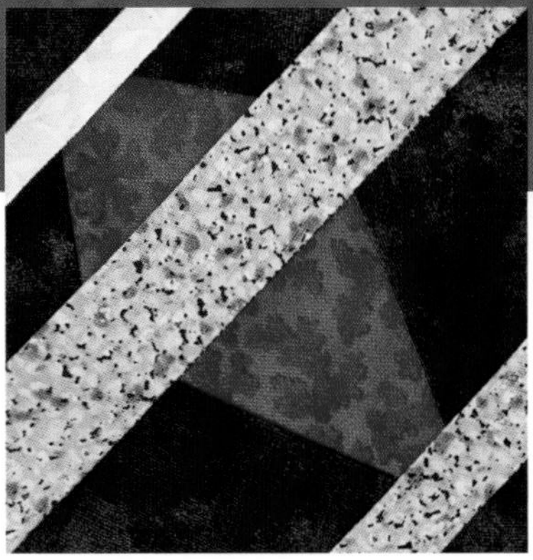

Fabric	Number to cut	Size to cut	Location
Blue	2	2¼″ × 3″	8, 9
	1	2¼″ × 2¼″ ◸	5, 11
	2	1½″ × 2″	2, 3
White	1	1″ × 3″	4
Red	2	2″ × 2″	1, 7
Gray	1	1½″ × 6″	6
	1	1″ × 3½″	10

◸ *Cut square; then cut it in half diagonally.*

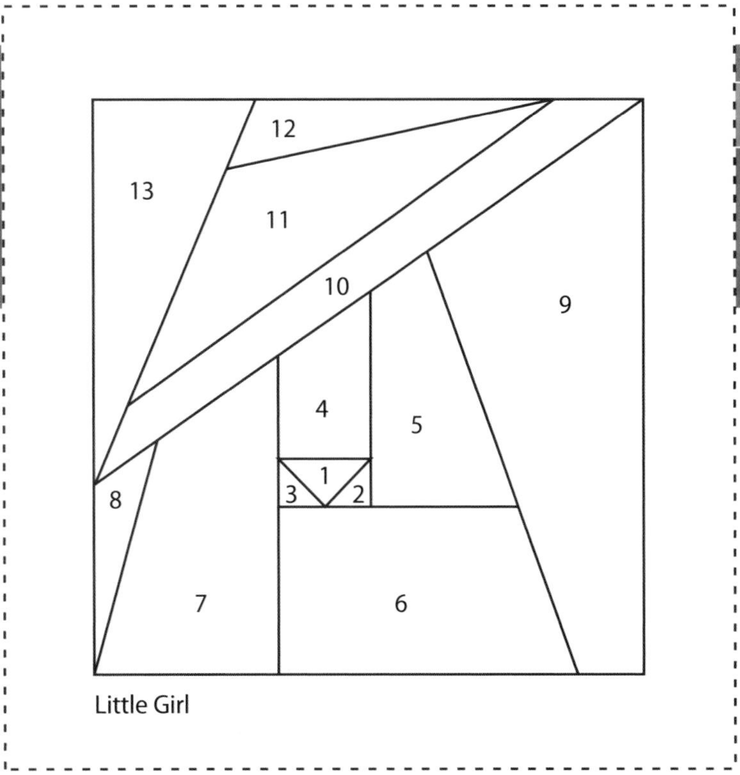

Little Girl

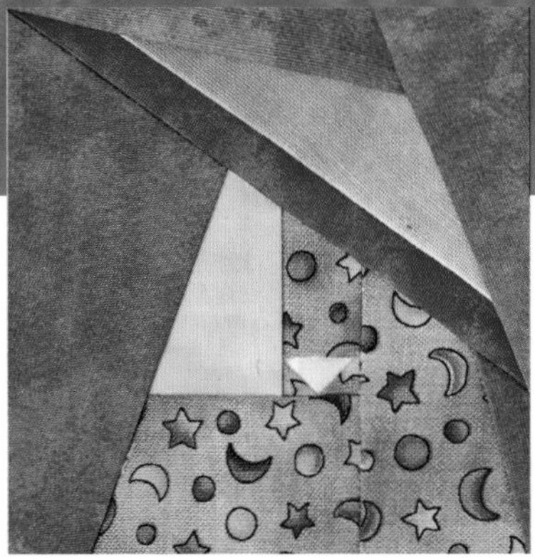

Fabric	Number to cut	Size to cut	Location
Blue	2	2¼″ × 4″	9, 13
	2	1″ × 3″	8, 12
Green	1	1½″ × 4″	11
Dark pink	1	1″ × 5″	10
White	1	1″ × 1″	1
Yellow	1	1½″ × 2″	5
Pink	2	2″ × 2½″	6, 7
	3	1″ × 1½″	2, 3, 4

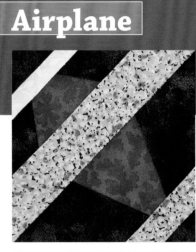

Rosebuds

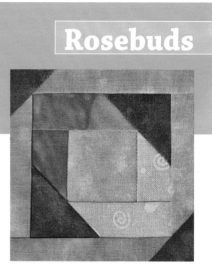

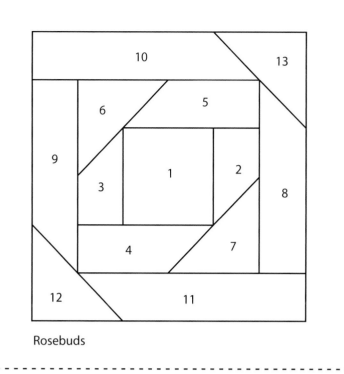

Rosebuds

Fabric	Number to cut	Size to cut	Location
Light green	1	1¾″ × 1¾″	1
	4	1¼″ × 3½″	8, 9, 10, 11
Pink 1	2	1¼″ × 2¼″	3, 4
Pink 2	2	1¼″ × 2¼″	2, 5
Medium green	2	2½″ × 2½″ ◺	6, 7, 12, 13

◺ Cut squares; then cut them in half diagonally.

Mailbox

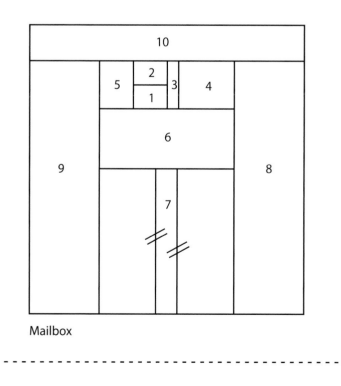

Mailbox

Fabric	Number to cut	Size to cut	Location
Green	3	1½″ × 4″	8, 9, 10
	2	1¼″ × 2½″	7
	3	1¼″ × 1¼″	1, 4, 5
Brown	1	¾″ × 2½″	7
White	1	1¼″ × 2¼″	6
Red	2	1¼″ × 1¼″	2, 3

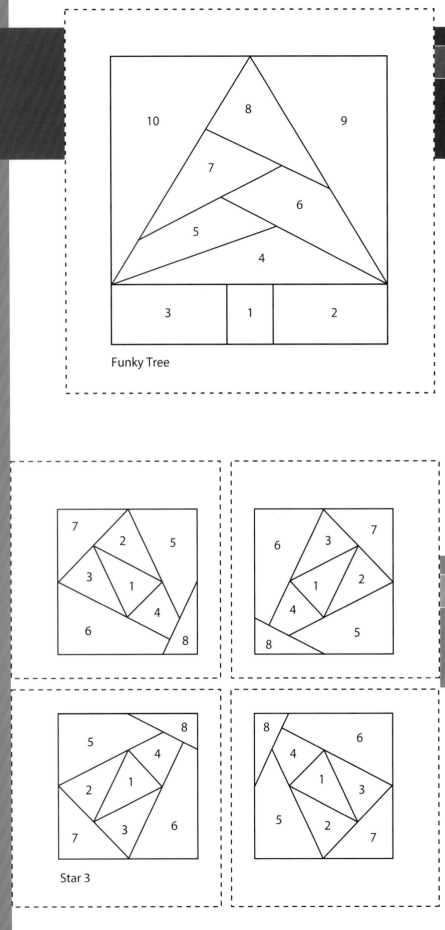

Funky Tree

Funky Tree

Fabric	Number to cut	Size to cut	Location
Black	2	2¼" × 4½"	9, 10
	2	1½" × 2"	2, 3
Brown	1	1¼" × 1½"	1
Green 1	1	1¼" × 4"	4
Green 2	1	1¼" × 3"	5
Green 3	1	1¼" × 3"	6
Green 4	1	1½" × 2½"	7
Green 5	1	1½" × 2½"	8

Star 3

Star 3

Fabric	Number to cut	Size to cut	Location
Maroon	2	2¼" × 2¼" 	7
	8	1½" × 2½"	5, 6
Teal	12	1½" × 1½"	2, 3, 4
Pink	4	1½" × 1½"	1
Beige	4	1¼" × 2"	8

 Cut squares; then cut them in half diagonally.

Love

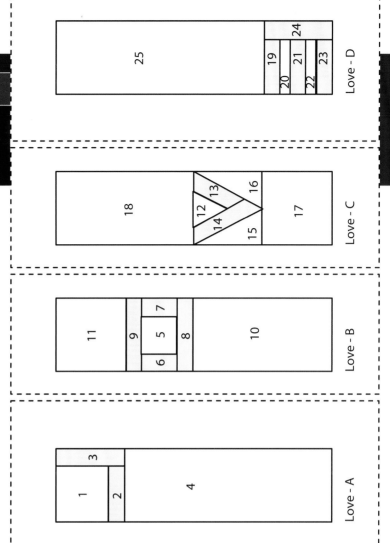

Love - D

Love - C

Love - B

Love - A

Fabric	Number to cut	Size to cut	Location
White	2	1¾″ × 3¼″	4, 25
	2	1½″ × 2½″	10, 18
	2	1¾″ × 1¾″	11, 17
	7	1¼″ × 1½″	1, 5, 12, 15, 16, 20, 22
Red	2	1″x 1½″	2, 3
Blue	4	1″ × 1½″	6, 7, 8, 9
Pink	2	1″ × 1½″	13, 14
Green	4	1″ × 1½″	19, 21, 23, 24

Basket 1

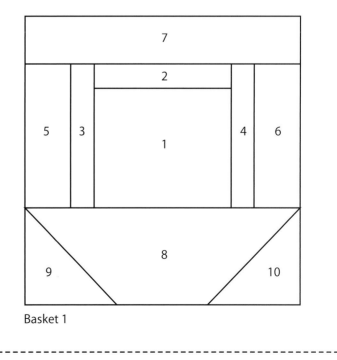

Basket 1

Fabric	Number to cut	Size to cut	Location
Floral	1	2″ × 2½″	1
Light green	1	1¾″ × 4″	8
	3	1″ × 2¼″	2, 3, 4
Dark green	1	2½″ × 2½″ ◺	9, 10
	3	1¼″ × 4″	5, 6, 7

◺ Cut square; then cut it in half diagonally.

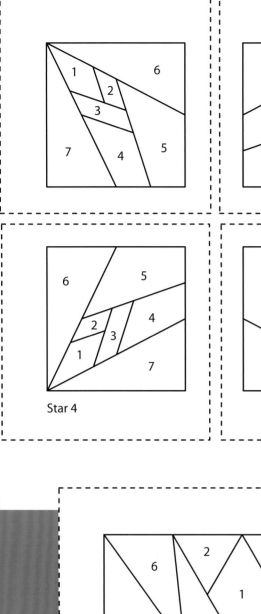

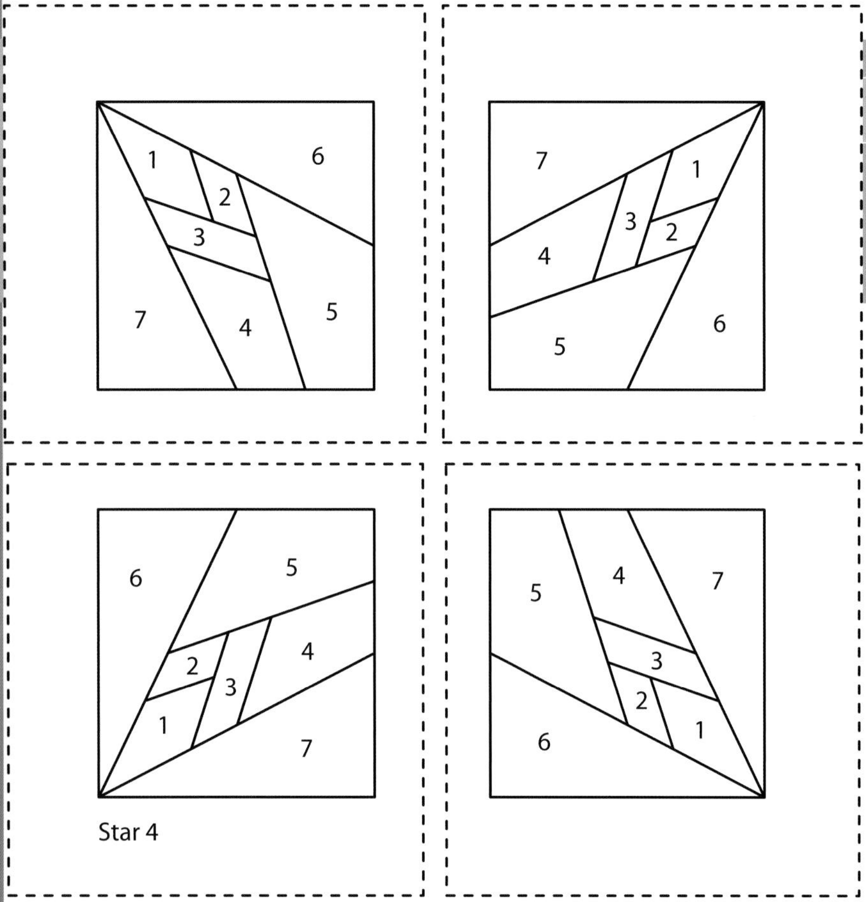

Star 4

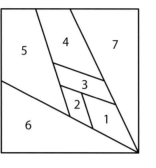

Fabric	Number to cut	Size to cut	Location
White/yellow	8	1½″ × 3″	6, 7
	8	1″ × 1½″	2, 3
Dark teal	4	1″ × 1½″	1
Medium teal	4	1¼″ × 1¾″	4
Light teal	4	1¼″ × 2¼″	5

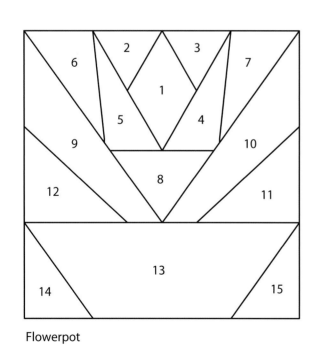

Flowerpot

Flowerpot

Fabric	Number to cut	Size to cut	Location
Light green	1	2½″ × 2½″ ◹	11, 12
	4	1½″ × 3″	6, 7, 14, 15
	3	1½″ × 2″	2, 3, 8
Dark teal	1	1½″ × 2″	1
Light teal	2	1¼″ × 2½″	4, 5
Blue	2	1¼″ × 3¾″	9, 10
Check	1	1¾″ × 4″	13

◹ Cut square; then cut in half diagonally.

Flower Trellis

Fabric	Number to cut	Size to cut	Location
Blue	1	2½″ × 2½″ ◺	13
	4	1¾″ × 3½″	6, 7, 10, 11
	2	1¼″ × 2¼″	2, 3
Yellow	1	1¼″ × 2¼″	1
Light purple	1	1¼″ × 2″	4
Purple	1	1¾″ × 2¾″	5
Light green	2	1¼″ × 3″	8, 9
Green	1	1½″ × 4½″	12

◺ Cut square; then cut in half diagonally.

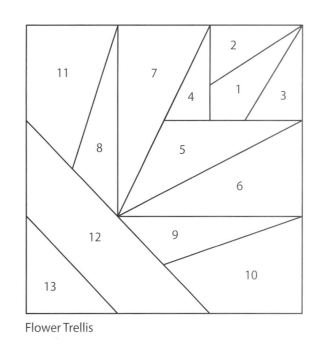

Flower Trellis

House

Fabric	Number to cut	Size to cut	Location
Blue	2	2″ × 3½″	11, 12
	2	1″ × 2½″	8, 9
Red	2	1½″ × 2½″	4, 6
	1	1″ × 3¼″	7
	2	1″ × 1¼″	2, 3
Black	1	2″ × 4″	10
	1	1¼″ × 2¼″	5
Yellow	1	1¼″ × 2″	1

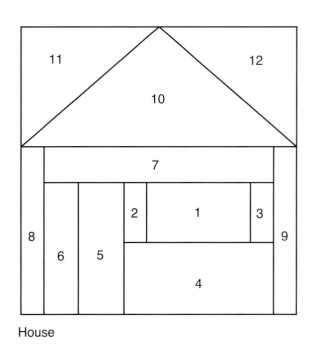

House

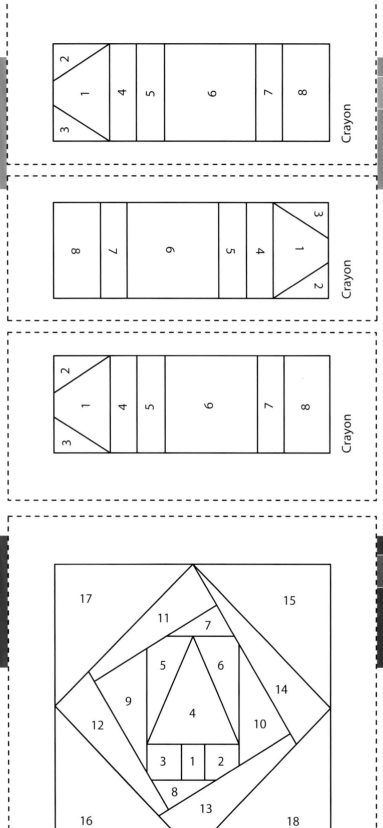

Crayons

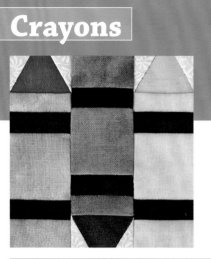

Fabric	Number to cut	Size to cut	Location
Light color	3	1¾″ × 1¾″	4, 6, 8
Medium color	1	1½″ × 1¾″	1
Black	2	1″ × 1¾″	5, 7
White	2	1″ × 2″	2, 3

The above cutting list is for 1 crayon color. Cut for red, blue, and yellow crayons.

Framed Tree

Fabric	Number to cut	Size to cut	Location
Dark peach	2	3″ × 3″ ◹	15, 16, 17, 18
Peach	4	1¼″ × 3″	11, 12, 13, 14
Dark green	4	1¼″ × 2″	7, 8, 9, 10
White	4	1″ × 2″	2, 3, 5, 6
Light green	1	2″ × 2″	4
Black	1	1″ × 1″	1

◹ *Cut squares; then cut them in half diagonally.*

Maple Leaf

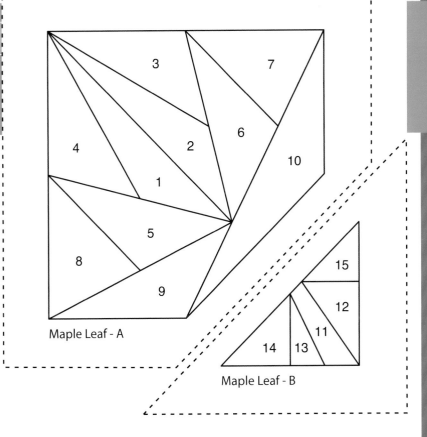

Maple Leaf - A

Maple Leaf - B

Fabric	Number to cut	Size to cut	Location
Blue	4	2″ × 3″	3, 4, 7, 8
	2	1¼″ × 2″	12, 13
Assorted fall colors	1	2½″ × 2½″ ◺	14, 15
	3	1½″ × 3″	5, 6, 9
	3	1¼″ × 4½″	1, 2, 10
Brown	1	1″ × 2″	11

◺ Cut square; then cut it in half diagonally.

Flag/Heart

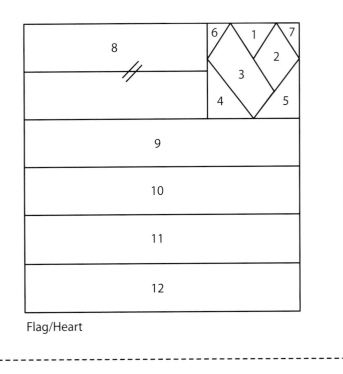

Flag/Heart

Fabric	Number to cut	Size to cut	Location
Red	2	1¼″ × 4″	9, 11
	1	1¼″ × 3″	8
White	2	1¼″ × 4″	10, 12
	1	1¼″ × 3″	8
	2	1″ × 2″	2, 3
Blue	5	1″ × 2″	1, 4, 5, 6, 7

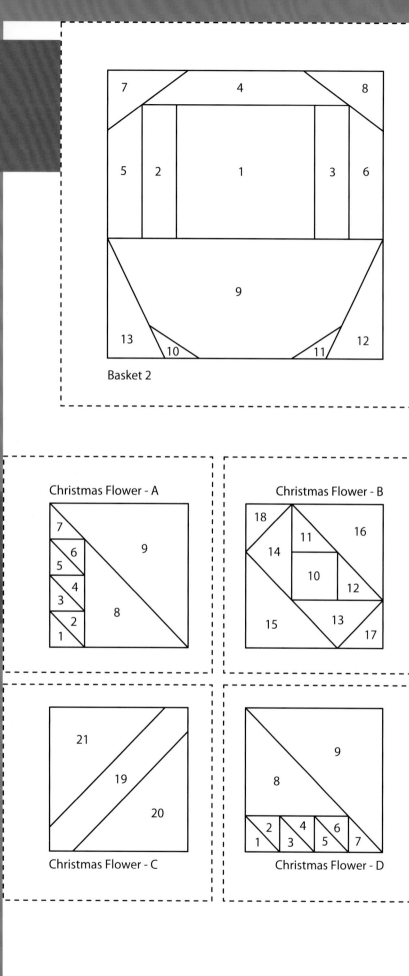

Basket 2

Fabric	Number to cut	Size to cut	Location
Light green	1	2¼″ × 2¼″	1
Beige	1	2″ × 4″	9
	3	1″ × 3″	2, 3, 4
Dark green	6	1½″ × 3″	5, 6, 7, 8, 12, 13
	2	1″ × 1½″	10, 11

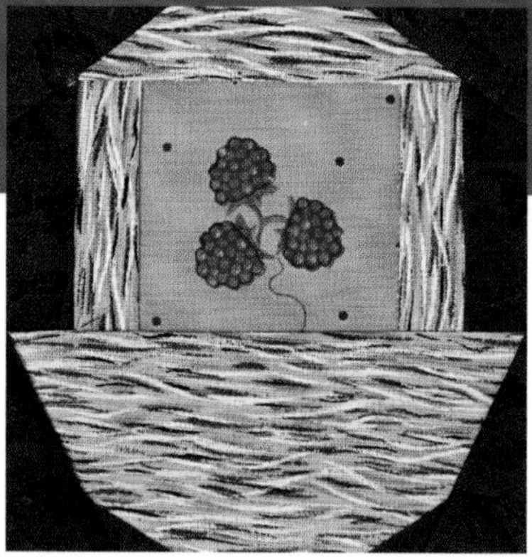

Christmas Flower - A

Christmas Flower - B

Christmas Flower - C

Christmas Flower - D

Christmas Flower

Fabric	Number to cut	Size to cut	Location
White	3	3″ × 3″ ◨	9, 16, 20, 21
	2	2″ × 2″ ◨	11, 12, 17, 18
	4	1¾″ × 1¾″ ◨	1, 3, 5, 7
Red	2	2½″ × 2½″ ◨	8, 15
	3	1¾″ × 1¾″ ◨	2, 4, 6
	1	1¼″ × 1¼″	10
Green	1	2¼″ × 2¼″ ◨	13, 14
	1	1″ × 3″	19

◨ *Cut squares; then cut them in half diagonally.*

Apple

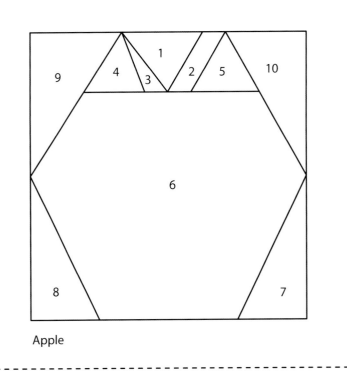

Apple

Fabric	Number to cut	Size to cut	Location
White	4	1½″ × 3″	7, 8, 9, 10
	3	1½″ × 1½″	1, 4, 5
Red	1	3″ × 3¾″	6
Green	1	1″ × 1½″	3
Brown	1	1″ × 1½″	2

Heart/Ribbon

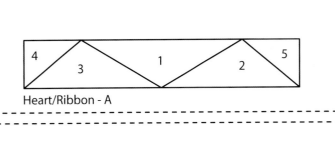

Heart/Ribbon - A

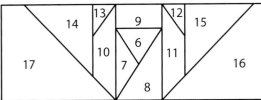

Heart/Ribbon - B

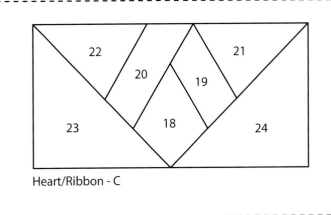

Heart/Ribbon - C

Fabric	Number to cut	Size to cut	Location
Green	2	3″ × 3″ ◻	4, 5, 23, 24
	1	1¼″ × 2½″	1
Yellow	2	2¾″ × 2¾″ ◻	14, 15, 16, 17
	5	2″ × 2¼″	2, 3, 18, 21, 22
	3	1″ × 1″	6, 12, 13
Pink	7	1″ × 2″	7, 8, 9, 10, 11, 19, 20

◻ *Cut squares; then cut them in half diagonally.*

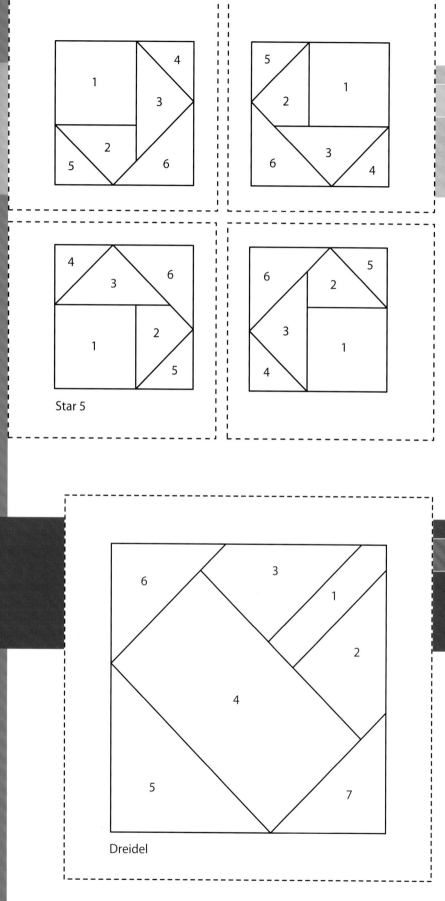

Star 5

Dreidel

Star 5

Fabric	Number to cut	Size to cut	Location
Blue	4	2¼″ × 2¼″ �	4, 5
	4	1¾″ × 1¾″	1
Yellow 1	2	2¼″ × 2¼″ ◪	6
Yellow 2	2	2¼″ × 2¼″ ◪	2
Yellow 3	2	2¼″ × 2¼″ ◪	3

◪ Cut squares; then cut them in half diagonally.

Dreidel

Fabric	Number to cut	Size to cut	Location
White	1	2¾″ × 2¾″ ◪	6, 7
	2	1¾″ × 2½″	2, 3
Dark red	1	2″ × 3¼″	4
Light red	1	3¼″ × 3¼″ ◪	5
Brown	1	1″ × 2½″	1

◪ Cut squares; then cut them in half diagonally.

Six-Pointed Star

Fabric	Number to cut	Size to cut	Location
Yellow	4	1½″ × 3″	7, 8
White	8	1½″ × 2″	2, 3, 5, 6
Blue	2	1½″ × 1½″	1
	2	1¼″ × 3½″	4

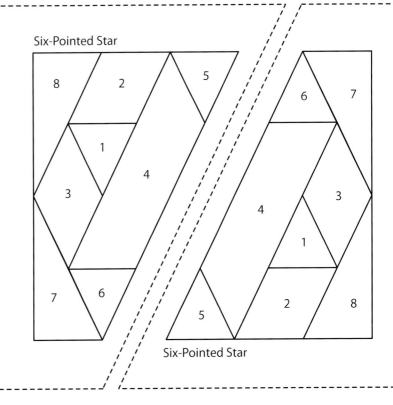

Six-Pointed Star

Six-Pointed Star

Candle

Fabric	Number to cut	Size to cut	Location
White	2	2″ × 3″	5, 6
	2	1½″ × 3″	8, 9
	2	1″ × 1¾″	2, 3
Yellow	1	1½″ × 1½″	1
Blue	1	1¼″ × 2¼″	4
Black	1	1½″ × 4″	7

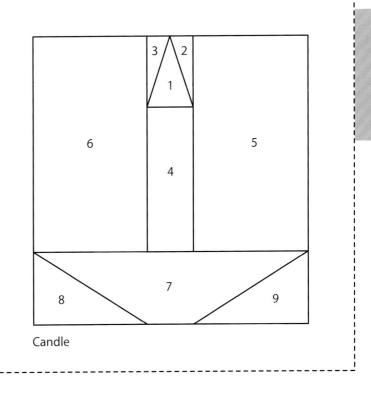

Candle

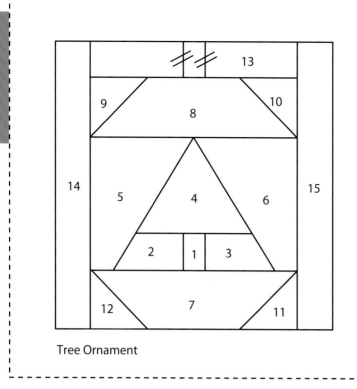

Tree Ornament

Fabric	Number to cut	Size to cut	Location
Red	4	1¾″ × 3″	5, 6, 7, 8
	2	1″ × 1½″	2, 3
Brown	1	1″ × 1″	1
Gold	1	¾″ × 1¼″	13
Green	1	1¾″ × 2″	4
White	2	2¼″ × 2¼″ ◹	9, 10, 11, 12
	2	1¼″ × 4″	14, 15
	2	1¼″ × 1¾″	13

◹ Cut squares; then cut them in half diagonally.

Gift

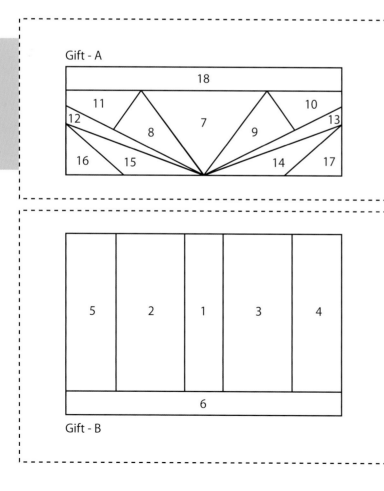

Gift - A

Gift - B

Fabric	Number to cut	Size to cut	Location
White	1	2″ × 2″ ◹	16, 17
	3	1½″ × 2¼″	4, 5, 7
	2	1½″ × 1½″	10, 11
	2	1″ × 4″	6, 18
	2	1″ × 2¾″	12, 13
Red	3	1″ × 2½″	1, 8, 9
Dark red	2	1″ × 2½″	14, 15
Green	2	1½″ × 2½″	2, 3

◹ Cut square; then cut it in half diagonally.

About the Author

Carol Doak discovered her love of quilting in 1979 when she took a seven-week basic quilting class in Worthington, Ohio. The following year she taught that class and discovered that she also loved to teach others how to make quilts. Since then she has taught more than a million people to quilt through her best-selling books and DVDs and by traveling to teach around the world.

Carol has elevated her trademark paper-piecing technique to levels not before seen in the world of quilting. Since writing her first paper-piecing book in 1993, Carol has created more than a thousand paper-pieced designs. Her passion for designing and teaching is evident to anyone who has taken a class from her or learned from her books and DVDs. She was named "Favorite Paper-Piecing Teacher" in 2008 by the readers of *Quilters Newsletter* magazine.

Carol lives with her family in Salem, New Hampshire, where the cold winters give her a reason to stockpile fabric—for insulation purposes!

Supplies/Resources

Carol Doak's Foundation Paper

Carol Doak's Keepsake Frame Cards
C&T Publishing, Inc.
800-284-1114
www.ctpub.com

Add-A-Quarter Ruler and Add-An-Eighth Ruler
CM Designs
303-841-5920
www.addaquarter.com

Rubber Stamps and Inks
Rubber Stamp Tapestry
336-879-6650
www.rubberstamptapestry.com

Carol Doak Newsletter and Web Page
www.caroldoak.com

Carol Doak Quilting Group
groups.yahoo.com/group/
CarolDoakQuiltingGroup

Products and books by Carol Doak

Great Titles *from* C&T PUBLISHING & STASH BOOKS

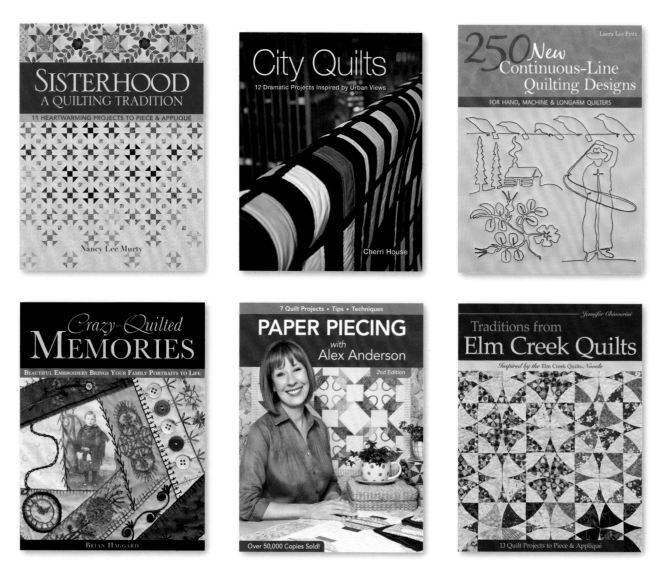

Available at your local retailer or **www.ctpub.com** *or* **800-284-1114**